Also by Toni Thomas:

Chosen
Fast as Lightening
Walking on Water
Blue Halo
Ace Raider of the Unfathomable Universe
You'll be Fast as Lightning Coveting my Painted Tail
Hotsy Totsy Ballroom
Love Adrift in the City of Stars
In the Pink Arms of the City
In the Kingdom of Longing
The Things We Don't Know
In the Boarding House for Unclaimed Girls
They Became Wing Perfect and Flew
Unburdened Kisses
Bandits Come and Remove Her Body in the Night
There is This
Here
The Smooth White Vanishing
Perishing in the Rain
A Different Measure of Moonlight
The Secret Language of River
Inside Her a River of Snow was Traveling
The Arbiter of Her Own Flame
Paradise on a Shoestring
A Bride of Amazement
A Portuguese Lullaby is What I am After

In the Hermitage of the Soul

Love Poems to Mexico

Published 2025
Annalese Press
West Yorkshire HD9 3XZ
England

Copyright © 2024 Toni Thomas

All rights reserved. No part of this publication may be reproduced, stored, or transmitted in any form, or by any means electronic, mechanical or photocopying, recording or otherwise, without the express written permission of the publisher.

Cover design and layout by Peter Wadsworth
El velo rojo, Red veil, Alexei von Jawlensky, 1912

British Library Cataloguing-in-Publication Data
A catalogue record for this book is available on request from the British Library.

ISBN 978-1-0685744-5-0

Part One *The Psalms of the Dark*

The man with the wounded bird	3
The girl spilling her life on the beach	4
In the square	5
My momie is peeling cucumber, onion	6
When trouble follows Lope	8
Our house	9
When my mother taught me	10
The psalms of the dark	11
When my auntie was named Pageant Queen	12
The child selling small treats	13
The horses in the parched field	14
At the patio café	15
My auntie has told me	16
Maria Gonzalez tells me	17
The man setting down the milk	19
The two barefoot children	20
Five houses from here	21
The young man	23
The young woman	25
On the ledge of the ditch	27

Part Two *In the Auction House of Frayed Space*

My father is worn boots	31
The potato sacks of the poor	32
Are some days salt and sea	33
The house of the dead holds room	34

My auntie claims	35
My cousin carries	36
My brother is stirring the batter	37
My father has a habit	38
My sister likes to ride	39
My mother is weaving	40
In the auction house of frayed space	41
My brother and I come here	42
It isn't easy	43
After dinner I rub the weary	44
At the Semana Santa	46
When I turned fifteen	47
Three streets down from here	48
My transistor radio	49
When part of me	50
My mother is calling to an invisible lover	51
When the rains come	52
One alley over	53
My birth mother says	54
If my mother comes	55

Part Three *When You Come*

My mother threw me a life jacket	59
The gardens of the dark	60
When you come	61
When your fever of birds	62
When you enter me	63
When the hurricane came	64
When the first child came	65
This day could feel like any other	67

The beach	68
Once I was beggar and mud	69
My mother's hands	70
My mother has aired out	71
My little sister	72
My grandmother's prayer book	73
I rub hope	74
In the yard	75
In the humid of evening	76
My mother is out in the field	77
When Candela hobbled into town	78
In this place laden with candles	79
My mother is folding the emptiness	80
This hour is ripe with melon	81
When the day	82
The hermitage of the soul	83

To love is to undress our names.
                Octavio Paz

*I have all that I lost and I go carrying my childhood
like a favorite flower that perfumes my hand.*
                Gabriela Mistral

Part One

The Psalms of the Dark

The man with the wounded bird

in his heart
has seen street vendors vanish
swallows eaten by poachers
fallen prophets
the palpitations of the moon shrink
has seen apartments turn into condos
the scant of a day laborer's wage
missing wife.

The man with the wounded bird
in his heart
won't talk about his oldest daughter
the tainted well
way things get broken
won't talk about his arthritis
how certain kinds of worship
can enslave.

He rises early
scrubs his face
eyes the world's crop shares
from the scant of his window
fries up two eggs
slips them into a tortilla
goes out into the dust and traffic.

The girl spilling her life on the beach

under a stubborn sun
is not looking for lovers
a penitentiary of desire that stings
like the scorpion in the grass
is looking forward to mealtime
the shade of a palm tree
burritos her mother has packed.

Does the girl spilling her life
remember the feather weight of hope
her mother sewed in her pocket
those first blue speckled eggs
imagine a time when no one needs
to walk back and forth on hot sand
hour after hour, day after day
offering to shiny bracelet your wrist
for a few pesos?

In the square

the day swells with buckets, coolers
songs of worship
swells with signs of the cross
children in bunny costumes
knowledge that Jesus must journey
pierce sorrow with his blood
rise up on the other side to save us.

In the square women braid hair
grill pork, peppers, onion
offer up soapstone dogs
rabbits, turtles for a few pesos
the sky washes the day of its razors
and the poor, the poor
who are plentiful
who out of the dust must make their home
lay their faces open
willing as an unclipped bud.

My momie is peeling cucumber, onion

not for us but for the taco stand
she runs with my popie.
All day he browns meat, chicken
peppers, onions over a hot flame
loads them into tacos
for a handful of pesos.

Popie claims if I watch my brother and sister
keep them from annoying anyone
he will buy me a motorized plane
that lifts like an eagle
claims if we work hard, really hard
we'll be able to move up hill
where there's less dust
the air is cleaner.

My parents like their parents
and the ones before
are handcuffed to Jesus
hang a cross, loop of rosary
over our front door so no one forgets.

Momie is cutting up lettuce, tomato
knows how to stretch things

clothes, meals, diapers
not ask for what won't arrive.

I am pinned like an olive to her branches
the fry pot of her stove.
Tell her – *I will never leave here*
but already she knows I will.

When trouble followed Lope

into the street
sucked up his well
swept away his oldest daughter
made limp the tomato vines
in a sea of drought

when trouble threatened to smash
his only glass window
steal the potato on his plate
it was no use feeding it sugar water
no use pretending life is just a party

when trouble persisted to find him
damp down the music in his ear
turn the faucet of his soul rusty
spill his net so the fish slipped out

Lope prayed the valley of his heart
would find room
always find room
even in a parched landscape

prayed his voice would still rise up
lift into god's singing
keep a place for the dead
the new born
to travel him.

Our house

is a scramble of salvaged wood
crumbled plaster
where children laugh
kick a cheap ball
eat without complaint
what is handed to them.

It is easy to assume
the weight of want
invades these walls
that the chicken on the grill
is always meant for someone else

easy to run your fingers across
the thin tablecloth
confirm what's missing

that come evening
sadness invades these rooms
my grandmother pines
father drinks to forget
mother's back is a rubbled field.

But then maybe faith
has no habit of deserting things
the levity of the heart
runs on more than sweat and money.
Still black birds sing in our tree
still the moon returns unbroken.

When my mother taught me

to strap on sandals, brush teeth
watch my brother for hours
taught me to grind corn
not ask for more than my share
I was too young to know
the world doesn't always listen
notice our worth

when my mother called my name
anointed me with her rope of rosary
showed me how to chop tomato, onion
turn the other cheek
what did I know of life
a small boy amid dusty rooms
a pounding sun
tourist crowded landscape

what did I know of endurance
how the soul must learn to sing
even in a moth eaten place
what did I know of my father's field
fallen to hard dirt
how the birds stay diligent
still mount our roof holy.

The psalms of the dark

are a red sky peopled with birds
the loyal farmer calming
the thirst of his lettuce
the summer voice of my mother
turning dust into a play toy.

Are some lives appetite and lament
a torn mesh married to Jesus
do they pocket the hard won pebbles
turn a stranger's face into friend?

When my auntie was named Pageant Queen

for the big parade over Semana Santa
my mama says the whole family teared up
helped her shop for a shiny tiara, chiffon dress
matching heels so high auntie nearly broke
her ankle on the cobbles.

My auntie is third generation beautiful
like her papa who had thick, silky black hair
far into his 70's and a peach smooth face.

Years later auntie still recalls
the crepe papered float drowned in confetti
fancy banquet with two roast pigs
how Manuel, her husband, courted her
with a clutch of daisies, clean linen suit
tells me that day the bells of the church
wouldn't shut up
in the tender of his eyes she was certain
the stir of god was calling.

Now every morning auntie flames the grill
in front of their apartment
coats her apron in spattered fat, heavy heat
grills pound after pound of chicken legs
loads them into foil buckets for the vendors.
She knows life can move fast, forget us
sets aside scrap for the stray dogs
tussles the hair of her children
waves them off to play with a kiss.

The child selling small treats

in a wicker basket
can't afford to think about bedtime
storybooks where frogs dine
fish escape
a girl turns into princess.

The child in shorts with bare feet
two missing teeth
knows how to make a world
out of dust and plastic
weave between tables of tourists
ask polite, walk away
when no one is listening
knows how to mind her mother
nurse the chipped stone in her pocket.

The mother hauls a metal rod
dangle of beaded earrings, pendants.
They are not expensive but nobody
seems eager to buy.

Where does their strength come from
how must it feel to move scant
amid the much?

The horses in the parched field

cannot scratch, tilt, move around
have their necks tethered to a short rein
as if any measure of freedom
is a foreign country.

Mornings and afternoons I walk by
witness their bound bodies
resignation
am reminded of cramped rooms
a crippled voice.

Who wills a horse to be bound
to a taut stake
with a bloodless fist?

Who will set them loose from
the wait to haul tourists
let them run, forage
stretch limb
nuzzle each other fearless?

At the patio cafe

I wipe my face of crumbs
find the torn side of Mary bleeding
stones, many stones
a past burdened with thorn fields.
My name spelt slant means *shy bird*.
At night rabbits forage these streets
as if the dark needs them.

At the patio café
pork sizzles in the kitchen
my lack of breeding holds a stained dress
I watch the tourist in the linen shirt
prick the skin of his dessert
its ribbon of blood red berries
wonder if he ever notices the way
poverty wears a thin slip
the mind can get lumbered
looking for answers.

At the patio cafe
the two women at the back
are loading a dishwasher, wiping down surfaces
laughing with each other
as if their bellies are a circus
as if back home no one needs to stretch rice
keep the children from school
for lack of enough money.

My auntie has told me

I am too big for my own good
eat her rooms out of rice and cake
tells me every man wants a shapely woman
bright pendant
till I feel less than the coins for our laundry.

It is not easy squeezing my life
into somebody else's version
being forced to dance salsa in a tight dress.

My auntie claims she only wants
what's best for me
a nice house, decent clothes
not being left to slave in a kitchen

that when my boat comes in
lithe and shapely
I will mount the rungs of sweet money
cultivate god amid the linens
silken and squeaky clean.

Maria Gonzalez tells me

she is never going to marry
give her life over to an unknown season
not with the sea calling
the light of her children's eyes
drawing her home.

She knows many things
how to shape fronds into a basket
thread seed beads intricate
stretch a pot of beans
so it spreads across three plates.

Maria's mother once told her
never leave your heart at somebody else's
doorstep as if your own is faulty
so she works to keep her heart safe
a clear star amid giants.

When Bonita Sanchez claimed
she was too high minded
for her own good
Maria didn't fling back words
just kept gutting her uncle's fish
wiped down the mischief till
it found a friend.

It was the time of the Semana Santa
when Christ suffers the cross

but promises to come back
when the women wait vigil
hold faith amid the stones.
Every night Maria's candle a lit flame.
Every night a chorus of bugs
pulsing beneath her window.

The man setting down the milk

for my coffee doesn't tell me
his hands are wearier than his heart's impulse
that the hurricanes of the dark can steal

doesn't talk about what happened to his wife
the apartment with the propane cooker
dusty motorcycle he once drove

doesn't tell me how old, how young he is
whether he dreams a new job, different life.

The man setting down the milk for my coffee
doesn't tell me he's a stranger to money
that vacations are for others
the ghosts of the past rise up

instead clears the next table
of its crumbs, empty plate
laughs with the other waiter
checks on enough toast

makes his shift into its own kind
of bright fiesta.

The two barefoot children

whose feet are the color of clay and longing
do not rest when the sun sleeps
go from table to table
offer up beaded necklaces, bracelets
baskets of foil wrapped treats
speak to strangers in the hope they will buy.
The mother hides the fallen moon in her face
she doesn't want her children to see.

The children carry the mother
the mother carries the children
amid tables of beer, margaritas
pizza, fish, fries, burgers
a blonde vocalist belting out tunes
gringos sucking ice cream.

Do the children, the mother go home
to a late night meal, comfy bed
stories, the promise of school time?
How must it feel to go about
anonymous as old people
forgotten pilgrims of the dust?

Five houses from here

is where the grudge started
over that fancy six burner gas grill
uncle claims he found tossed in a heap
off the Guerro Road on the track
that leads to Monkey Mountain
says it is his by consent
since nobody else claimed it.
He has rid the rust, screwed back legs
turned the grill into something special.

But that's not the story of Jose G.
who says uncle is greedy, stole it from
Lorella, his second sister
grabbed it right off her patio at night
when nobody was looking.
Says his sister got it from the Costco
thanks to a gift card from her aunt.
It's her prize grill
she would never dump it
wants it back.

Now uncle and Jose don't speak
pop open beer cans.
His other sister Sophia likes to gossip
so the whole village is talking a storm
over Lorella's tears, her fancy gas grill
from Costco that's been stolen.

My papa claims that's what happens
when want takes over, crowds the soul
till there's no room for a half starved donkey
says meat will never brown decent
on a grill lumbered with cruel words
a bucket load of resentment.

The young man

who carries a rose in his heart
is hungry for the scent of April.
He has never known much money
but still the day hums with promise
still his mother wakes early
feeds the chickens
set his beans on the stove.

The young man lives above the
taco stand on Hubero Road
where dust coats thick
where he has lived for twelve years
with two sisters, an aunt, his parents and four dogs.
The dogs do not belong to them
but still come around at mealtime
in the hope of scrap.

The boy knows the sea
knows the jungle
the welts on his father's hands
the work of hauling –
bricks, bags of sand, crushed concrete
knows that life doesn't come easy
there are burdens even god must carry

but still he tucks hope into his pocket
still the sea listens
offers up its tides of shell, seaweed

still the tourists come, go
the stars know him
still his mother swoops him up
reminds him
we are each of us
precious.

The young woman

in the square of Sayulita
is not searching for love or money
just sways her arms, cups the air
as if god is a fountain
her words have been swept dry
in a clear stream.

She has a midriff top, streaked hair
twisted into dreadlocks
looks like a Scandinavian model
her face soft, tan, peach stained
her body a succulent tree
likes to kiss the face, neck of her boyfriend
run her arms up and down his back and tummy.
He has long dark ropes of hair
shorts with no top, is copper skinned
very thin, speaks soft tones of English
says he comes from a southern province.

Every day all hours they inhabit the park.
The man sits at times behind a blanket
clothe covered in crystals
tells me for six months they stayed in the jungle
lived off herbs, fruit.
The crystals are small but lovely.
He only accepts donations
trusts the universe to provide.

But it is their daughter I watch most.
She is about two, sun stained
wobbly as she wanders the busy square
in her loose cotton dress
fingers an empty plastic bottle
cries to be picked up.
What will she eat come mealtime?
When tiredness turns cranky friend
where will she go
where does she sleep?

On the ledge of the ditch

that in another season holds rain
bulges fast and furious
murky with spillage

on the ledge of the ditch
that is now parched dirt
the frame of old pickups
where I met my first girl
the one in the petaled dress
who dusted my lips with honey

on the ledge of the ditch
where day vendors set up their stalls
offer jewelry, rattles, blankets, pottery
where the prices are cheap
everybody wants a bargain

on the ledge of the ditch
away from the frenzy
the patio bars, street music, tourists
I come to sit in the dusk
turn the world quiet

contemplate
how the words of god
hang on such a thin thread
such a thin thread
so many things get broken.

Part Two

In the Auction House of Frayed Space

My father is worn boots

scabby legs, a sea of regret
sawdust and brick
his crushed lunch pail

my father is the dry hills of Conchuilla
dust wiped off his marriage
the pop of beer cans
his lost mother
the insistence of flies.

My father is the plod of foot soldiers
many leavings, welcome backs
words he's forgotten
crumpled ones he clings to.

Come nightfall
you can see him climbing
climbing, climbing
the hillside of his regrets
with a lit cigarette
begging the sky to speak mercy
in the name of Jesus.

When you come
wash my father's hair in your bucket
will my father kneel
not complain
turn away such gift
in the name of want?

The potato sacks of the poor

weigh more than bags of coin
weigh a day laborer's scant pay
the dust of their children
weigh the weight of want
in a forgotten place.

To sip their lot is to know
dirt and salt
a blue rosary
handholding.

All summer the heat threatens to strangle
birds shelter in the tree
mama dusts off my brother's sandals
straightens my pale ribbon
for the Sunday mass.

Are some days salt and sea

a yellow ball tossed for the stray dog
back and forth, back and forth
throw and retrieve, game time

are some days washed up cuttlefish
too many vendors
the postponed wedding
lace rubbed against mud
steak then beans
sweat and handholding
too many beers, a hangover?

Are some days a rusted motorcycle
place with no name, name calling
rotted fruit married to tequila
the creased hands of my mother
rolling out the tortillas

are some days a substitute
handstands and pose
to keep the rent money coming
faith stuffed inside a hanky?

The house of the dead holds room

always holds room
my mama told me.
No one goes thirsty for lack of care.

But it takes sturdiness
to memorize this message
tuck it in my heart as if
the day holds no tyrants

as if enough beans and rice
will always arrive
nobody aches from laying
too much rock, concrete.

The house of the dead holds room
always holds room
my mama told me
like inside the shirt of Jesus
the virgin mother with her net
like Carlos and Rouel up on the roof
feeding the pigeons
out of the nothing in their pocket.

My auntie claims

at the rate I am going
I will rot my teeth with candy
nobody wants to court a girl
squeezed into tight shorts.

But she doesn't know
god walks through my rooms
parading a different sunset

beauty can be fickle
prone to vanish
not all of us need to shine neon
haul our voice
big as a loudspeaker.

My cousin carries

the weight of the village on his back
its drought, hunger, sunken rooms
carries a peasant's sunset
beans, tomato, squash
prays the rains will return
the sun makes no penitentiary
out of the moon's hymnbook.

My cousin is my aunt's oldest
the one with the petaled birthmark
who lets no one starve for lack of trying.
Aunt claims he has luck riding on his side
but the world is blind, doesn't see.

For a wage my cousin shovels gravel, sand
goes mile upon mile while his feet ache
shoulders attempt to keep steady
the voice of Jesus.

For the neighbors he hauls corn
sorghum, millet, tables and chairs
but will this be enough?

My brother is stirring the batter

for pancakes
will spill in a cup of berries
when the mix is smooth
just as my mother instructs.

He is only seven, prone to mishaps
a broken arm from climbing the roof
stitches after poking the window fan
with his middle finger.
My mother prays he will smarten up.

My brother doesn't yet live
by sums of money
button his heart shut to keep
the day from stealing
doesn't yet know poverty can be a
whip in a windstorm.

It will take years, many places
for the world to catch up.

My father has a habit

of rescuing spiders, mice
scary bugs
wants them to roam free
have a better life.

It's not easy for him
feeling like a spare part
blue orphanage
tank topped body
anchored to brick.

My father strokes geckos
hairless dogs
the strays that follow him
in hope of scrap.
For how many years
have his arms ached
for how many years
has he married a thin plate
looking for Jesus?

My father rescues hairy creatures
moves them out into the dirt
while I watch
doesn't like to harm things
appear too soft.
Is it good he keeps his fears private
amid the world's bulldozers?

My sister likes to ride

a carnival horse with no name
believes it is hers
the polished blue saddle
gold braiding
crank that lifts her up and down
round and round.

My sister doesn't yet know poverty
how it can stuff a worm in your pocket
doesn't yet know about hours and hours
hauling baskets, handbags, jewelry, melon
on the beach without any shade

how not everyone gets to attend school
tuck into a lunchbox
learn math, science, poems

doesn't yet know the world carries want
not every future holds a spaceship.

My mother is weaving

the soul of the dark into our dinner
her body's ripe fruit
weaving three parts spring
a memory of birth

doesn't count on a well-paid job
luck to save us
believe the world carries only silt
a rich person's epistle.

My mother prays her man will stay loyal
our broken window gets fixed
stray dogs stop tearing into the garbage

prays the night sky will remember
offer up slices of melon
a constellation of stars
not spit.

In the auction house of frayed space

when my soul turns weary
the sign of the cross
feels like an empty vow

it is then that the neighbors
are likely to arrive
with their chips
beans, rice, salsa

kiss me as if even in
a pinched landscape
children sing
the sky knows no limit
birds never brow beat

kiss me
as their one and only.

My brother and I come here

to outrun a thin plate
imagine steak and ice cream
a silvered river
boatload of fish.

My mother sprinkles our foreheads
in holy water
while my father waits.

Is it for her
I mount this cross
marry my broken wings
to Jesus?

It isn't easy

to travel a road of stone
watch others drink from the well
while our own sits empty

isn't easy to mop hotel floors
launder dozens of bed sheets
haul buckets day after day
mount the cross willing
accept a scant plate
while my children wait

isn't easy to turn the other cheek
not make want into a high rise
circle the dirt, the dust
around and around
keep my face
my heart swept

accept this day
this hour
your voice as enough.

After dinner I rub the weary

out of my grandmother's feet
slosh them in a bowl of salted water.
She wants me to do this
wants me to act decent
the good girl in a sea of candy.

My grandmother's hair is black sand
married to silver
twisted up with a plastic clip
so she can work no nonsense.
For years she has sold soda
milk, eggs, bananas, beans
from our kitchen window
been called *the stubborn goat* by my popie
for the way she refuses the word *no*
with the flap of her apron.

My grandmother's stories are half vinegar
half rosemary, an ammunition of Jesus
loaves of bread in the desert.
Her hands hold fern, arroyos
the hunger of birds
the beach swept clean
after autumn's hurricane.

Has my grandmother stolen my tongue
drowned it in her own river
now that stray dogs wander my soul

anxious to be fed?
Have I become an empty room
tethered to her Jesus?

At the Semana Santa

the priest gathers palms
that swell with Christ's blood
clears the day of its thorns
while we kneel.

At the Semana Santa
Jesus is forced to carry a cross
hang from it
testify to what it means to stay loyal
be broken, rise up
while the women weep.

Up the street
tourists down plates of eggs benedict
toast, sausage, omelet
buy clay pots, rattles, silver
coconut mats painted in villages
green hills and hope.

At the Semana Santa
I wash my mouth of its fish hooks
finger a blue rosary
pray you will purge my heart
of its rock fields.
Know the world alone won't save.

When I turned fifteen

it was a big deal
relations threw a huge party
enchiladas, gossip, piñata, cake
loud music, lots of beer.
I got to dress up
dance with my father and uncle
sip my first margarita.

When I was fifteen
I was told if I keep my head straight
heart tethered to Jesus
every manner of good will arrive
suck up the world's rock fields.

My girlish shorts were handed down
to my middle sister
a couple of curvy dresses took
their place in the closet.

When I turned fifteen
I anchored you to my table
asked you to mend bruises
my mother's periled voice
bring the risen of Easter
to every tear stained hankie
fallen wish.

Three streets down from here

my father is burning his body
slow
year after year, day after day
even as the arroyos call his name
my mother sits patient.

Three streets down from here
my father is splashing his face
burning his body
in a chorus of bricks
back ache.

Who will come to him
in the hour of need
when his lungs are choked
the ocean can't find him

who will lessen the load
wash his feet in the name of Jesus
come to my mother
in the thick hour of her wait?

My transistor radio

is washing over your cooler, blanket
the beach's wet curve
with a frenzy of strings
asks you come to attention
notice.

All week I have waited for you
to search the stations of my face
my body's cool breeze
inked with seagulls.

My transistor radio is swooning
a rhapsody of birds
calling the fruit of your heart
from its tree.

Why stay pinned forever
while the waves sing
my orange sunset beckons
to drown you
in a valley of flame?

When part of me

wants more than squalor
more than work and work
more than a dust choked road
wants fishnet stockings
a paisley dress that shows legs

when part of me wants sirloin
a trip to Mazatlan
plates of grilled octopus
the shawl in the shop window
hounded by sequins

when the going gets rough
there's only scraps for the supper
I try to imagine the world different
nobody needing to beg
hoist their bodies day after day
into exhaustion

imagine my life risen
the train not needing to speed
sunlight generous across the cobbles
yellow finch high in the tree
the old man on the bench smiling
awnings of shade that sing.

My mother is calling to an invisible lover

who sleeps in her memory
doesn't need to get drunk
to remember Jesus
doesn't need to pursue other women
as if his own is a relic
doesn't demand more than
the scant at our table.

My mother is calling
not to her youth
not to our times to save
but this invisible lover
who looks beyond plastic
will scoop us up
beyond the half buried tomb
remember.

When the rains come

knee deep
thick as a swollen vow
when they come
not partial to money
not partial to you, to me

don't say I will turn away
shrink from the menace of death
only tally up my losses

don't say my mother
will desert the past
forget to call my name
out of the drowned forest

no, tell me
I will meet this onslaught
with the moist of my lips.

One alley over

where the cobbles are buckling
where motorcycles, hungry dogs
thin chickens wander
amid the bright arms of children

one alley over
where I travel with the dust
plastic bottles, blankets, trinkets
with those us who must turn the
earth's hard clay into a paycheck

one alley over
where a spatter of shaved rooms
paw the hill
where the cats search garbage
I imagine Jesus right now
at one of our small tables
tucking into a plate of beans, rice
laughter.

My birth mother says

I am a sack of cloth
in need of mend
god never sets foot
in an unwept room
burdened with clutter.

She was born in a season
of famine, gnarled roots
bruised fingers.

One day when August melts
will you rise up in me
hold my voice as a chalice
will the geckos call my name
not as the girl who palsies the moon
but who's fruitful?

If my mother comes

with her armload of corn, melon
not to stab the day
but turn it swollen
will your body open slow
the wealth of its cargo
your clothes mind no
measure of conceit
treason?

If my mother comes
will you see her
as more than the woman
who pins laundry
skillets potato
hoses down children
sweats in a sea of labor

offer up your lips
the world's sweetness
come to her broken open
as psalm?

Part Three

When You Come

My mother threw me a life jacket

orange as fish swimming
a mist broken over the sea's fitful.

My mother wished for me
a life with less holes
not this sinking
sinking away.

Why does she mind
these floors that I weep on
why is my body not really my own
but her arms
her voice
coming back to me?

The gardens of the dark

are washing my hair
with their voice
the prayer songs of Jesus.

Who is to say when the
day reeks of blind
I must follow?

Who wipes the sweat
of our brows
our bodies
in the moon's wade pool?

When you come

please bring salt
plump tomatoes
bright strands of ribbon
please bring your heart
not in a mason jar
but clear

when you come
rattle my blinds open
undress my seams
that have supped with winter
but are determined to rise

when you come
please forgive the mess
crumbs on our table
the way my voice pits and pines
like a storybook only half open

when you come bearing your cross
don't assume I will forget forever
be the anxious bride in a sea of brine

when you come
know I want to stay faithful
for so long became lost.

When your fever of birds

travel my sky's blue basin
the sun's forensic
travel midnight
with its torn stockings
angular mapmaking

when they move past linguistics
to a language of faith
that is more than feather
bound in the trees

then will the blurred
of my body lament
take up your glory
spring commotion
penchant for lovemaking?

When you enter me

clear away the rubble
pronounce me
your *one and only*

when you enter me
calm the tides
offer up beans and rice
at my soul's tray table

when you come
divested of rules
wash over me
a summer day
burdened with nothing

let me not eye the past
find it wanton
but offer you up everything
my warts and roses

blaze my body, my face
soft
as your newly lit cathedral.

When the hurricane came

September and the tourist season not yet begun
when it came
stripped the beach of its lounge chairs, bodega
littered with debris, tree limbs, torn metal
washed up cans, coolers, fish, seaweed

turned the hunger of squalid rooms into chaos
when it came, drove my uncle from his sleep
to try and save things – the taco stand, grill
plates, buckets, his father's boat
when it came, drove my mama to wake us
huddle up close

when the hurricane came
when I was no longer waiting around
for god
braiding my hair neat to please him
when it came
loss after loss after loss

when things started to unravel
I began to relearn Jesus
the weight of the cross
women at the well
accept so much gets broken
yet somehow we are willed
to come back.

When the first child came

everyone was happy
bells rang through the room
like a valley of blossom
and then the second
then the third
so many mouths to feed
on a thin paycheck
so much milk, flour
beans, shoes, rent.

When the first came
she was named Marianna
girl of the sea
as if all the others afterwards
would drink from her
stay nourished.

Marianna of the holy sea.
Marianna of the torn dress
worn-down sandals.
Marianna who ties her hair in a rope
walks the beach back and forth
offers up cups of watermelon, papaya.

You can see the joy of the sunbathers
some fat, some thin, some brown
some white, some old, some young

when they hand over their pesos
lift her juicy red and orange pulp
to their lips.

This day could feel like any other

the sun high in the sky
a coat of dust blinding the cars
stray dogs out in the street
searching for scrap
the palms regal as if dignity
is an inborn friend.

I am wiping my face
but then there is so much to wipe
like the wants that infest me
this day, this hour
being precious

my face a constancy that looks back
not in disbelief of the mysteries
that wait to descend
but in wonder at what we survive
what anchors with a silent thread.

The beach

at the end of this jungle trail
is not looking for mercy
doesn't need to fan its face
perfume the sand with wet kisses
in the hope you will come
is not looking for a fantasy lover
tide prone to only big and fearsome

doesn't mind if you do or don't
pause to listen, sit on the rocks
unwrap your sandwich
witness the three stray dogs
sand crabs
quiver of shells

the beach at the end of this trail
isn't preening her silvered surface
in the name of perfect
won't boast waters so lukewarm
they can vouchsafe a child
cure your sickbed
absolve hurts, the future

the beach at the end of this trail
knows that no cell phone map
myriad of footsteps
may be enough
to arrive.

Once I was beggar and mud

the disguised petal
squalored myself in the shade of giants.
To eat at my table was to know
complaint, gossip
stone throwing.

But that was before the drought set in
the one that hollows bones
the cornfield
turns a stray dog empty.

That was before I remembered
the sounds of your jungle
hidden path to the beach
where waves come like flame
repeat and repeat

remembered that
to give myself over
is to be found.

My mother's hands

hose cool water over
the parched of my day
are the petaled napkin at a
soiled dinner party

my mother's hands
are a mission of eggs, potato
the day of my birth
sewn in her palm

are memory making
forgiveness
swept dirt
the clatter of cook pans

my mother's hands
are five parts sympathy
a worn smock
fondness for tomatoes.

She has spent years
scooping up leftovers
chinks of sunset
diligent
keeping them safe.

My mother has aired out

my room of its sickbed
aired out my blue steeples
till the April of springtime
can find space
a meadow with rosebuds.

What would I be without
her damp eye laying bare
the sky's night purse
the sun's vigilance?

See how she comes to me
in this year of the goat
purges my heart
till I am more than provocation
become lamplight
seed
the splash of her voice calling.

My little sister

reorders rooms
my father's voice till it
echoes her springtime.

I thank her
for my feathered thread
summer ice
dinner trays under the palm tree

thank her for bugs, rain songs
taming the creatures of the dark
with her flame.

My little sister traffics
in sick rooms
a hidden door
forest unburdened by giants.

My grandmother's prayer book

holds consecrated wine
a red paper dress, lit candles
holds a hen house
dungarees on a sloped line
rooms undeterred by money
holds a girl once held hostage
made to shrink small as a bug

my grandmother's prayer book
holds hearsay
the annunciation of rain
sun's eyelet
frayed rope turned rescue
many fish.

When I come
she takes out her knife
not to stab the dead weight
of my rock fields
but to slice the fruit for our lunch.

For how many years
have strayed dogs waited
for scrap by her table
for how many years like me
have they come away grateful?

I rub hope

into my heart's blue basin
rub in salt so I can
carry the ocean
carry my mother's kisses

rub in determination
my steeled body
the soft of milled corn
magnolia.

Who is to say the
day is stale
a thin lamppost
when I walk
the path of stones
handcuffed to you?

In the yard

the tangled overgrown part
where the three mangy dogs wait
where papa has set up his portable grill
and mama says the weeds are crushing

in the backyard
where Lido likes to pee
and I lost my one and only
plastic poodle keychain

mama and papa sit out the evening
in their fold out chairs.
They are not old, not young
have fingernails mapped with
the dirt of heavy loads
the hard won love
they keep for each other.

And it is here I come when
I am out of sorts
my day is dust and bricks
a nameless sun calling

it is here I come
not to lament
our runt of a garden
dig up useless words
pronounce the world *broken*
but just to watch.

In the humid of evening

you wait
call me out of the dust
burdens of money
mischief

remind that sweetness is more
than the meat of the guava
shiny words
day winding its web
of greed and forgetful.

Out of the cool breeze
tangle of jungle
half notes, pebbled road
you call to me

sister my shoes
sister my room with its peeled walls
sister my lover, children
so that when the rains come
the hurricane threatens

I am *not* alone
stay blessed.

My mother is out in the field

carrying the drought on her shoulders
pressing the wrinkled folds of our dirt
to her dream of sheep.

My mother is pinned to poems
from a saint's prayer book
wants to avert our terrible fate
raise the faro, tomatoes, corn
out of their deathbed.

My mother is seeding our day
with her tears
using her arms to sweep the sky
in the name of god's thunder

calling the stray dogs back
for their scraps of supper

calling, calling, calling
in the name of you
in the name of me.

When Candela hobbled into town

for the Semana Santa
her hair twined in a rope of ribbon
came with her dusty shoes
thin life

it is true god was waiting
quiet but steady
the weight of some stone lifted
her weathered hands
found a new embrace.

Afterwards neighbors marveled
over her combed out sorrows
softened face
the way street dogs protect

her voice had become
a well of water
unclaimed by winter.

In this place laden with candles

with the memory of ant, star, tree
my mother is wiping my feet with her tears
with her words that are salt and river
the silver bellies of fish preening

is wiping my grief's fallen hem
laying her body down thick
as an altar.

In this place laden with candles
my mother is wiping my feet
calling me home
to a different song

till only her voice remains
and these candles
burning
burning
burning
my wants to ash.

Who would I be to turn away
such gift in the dark?

My mother is folding the emptiness

of the night into my being
bribing the moon, huge in the sky
to act as a flashlight
is winging a flight of birds
in my direction
the scent of cow dung
jasmine.

Is it out of a chipped pail
I come to her
or because she has been
calling, calling
calling me back
insistent
till my words are more fountain
than flint
the dark releases its tyrants

till I am the bright
in her beam
dancing?

This hour is ripe with melon

stained sandals
a woman twining palm fronds
is memory and forgetting
the sizzle of red peppers
stray dogs pawing at garbage

this hour is beach tans and surfboards
pinned sheets, trousers
a wishing bone for what's to come
what's been lost

this hour is the itch of bug bites
two boys with squirt guns
a plastic bottle left in the dirt

this hour is lament and soothsaying
the crumple of a bulldozed house
dust hosed down, then come back

this hour is the cleaning of hands
the cleaning of hearts
the path less taken
the secret one we almost forgot.

When the day

is three parts fantasy
and a plate of rice

when it rises a steep slope
of work and weight

when the beach is cluttered
with want and tourists

the hours many
the rest small

then you travel into my heart's suitcase
gift me with moist kisses
an apothecary of birds.

The hermitage of the soul

is part soiled hem
a chorus of rain rattling
the windswept beach
child turning dust
into a tortilla
gulls, many gulls.

The hermitage of the soul
is beyond power or money
runs on slow time
takes the day's longing
backache, worn shoes
turns them into an altar
gift of peaches

sups at the poor man's table
holds the rope of a woman's
rosary like a bride.

Toni Thomas lives in Portland, Oregon. Her poems have been published in Austria, Spain, New Zealand, Canada, England, Scotland, and Australia. In the United States her work has appeared in over fifty literary magazines including *Prairie Schooner, North Dakota Quarterly, Hayden's Ferry Review, the Minnesota Review, Notre Dame Review, Poetry East*, and more. She has been twice nominated for a Pushcart prize, and won several awards. She has published twenty-five collections of poetry and six books for children.

Her figurative clay sculptures have been shown in gallery exhibits in Portland and Chicago, displayed in literary magazines, and housed in private collections in the U.S. and England.

Her short documentary *One of Us* was shown at the Trans-ideology: Nostalgia festival in Berlin and at the Museum of Contemporary Art in Taipei.

Since Toni loves to create and sits buried in reams of poems, manuscripts, clay figures and images….she likes to imagine all of them out in the world
swaying wild as the lupine.

tonithomaspoetry.com